Derrida, an Egyptian

Derrida, an Egyptian

On the Problem of the Jewish Pyramid

PETER SLOTERDIJK

TRANSLATED BY WIELAND HOBAN

polity

First published in French as *Derrida, un Égyptien* © Maren Sell Éditeurs, Paris, 2006. Translated from the original German text.

This English edition © Polity Press, 2009

Polity Press
65 Bridge Street
Cambridge CB2 1UR, UK

Polity Press
350 Main Street
Malden, MA 02148, USA

ISBN-13: 978-0-7456-4638-1 (hardback)
ISBN-13: 978-0-7456-4639-8 (paperback)

A catalogue record for this book is available from the British Library.

Designed and typeset in 12/17pt ITC Garamond Light
by Peter Ducker MISTD

Printed and bound in Great Britain
by MPG Books Limited, Bodmin, Cornwall

The publisher has used its best endeavours to ensure that the URLs for external websites referred to in this book are correct and active at the time of going to press. However, the publisher has no responsibility for the websites and can make no guarantee that a site will remain live or that the content is or will remain appropriate.

Every effort has been made to trace all copyright holders, but if any have been inadvertently overlooked the publishers will be pleased to include any necessary credits in any subsequent reprint or edition.

For further information on Polity, visit our website:
www.politybooks.com

Contents

Acknowledgements

I would like to take this opportunity to thank Daniel Bougnoux, who told me during an encounter in Villeneuve-les-Avignons about the event 'A Day of Derrida', which was planned for 21 November 2005 at the Centre Pompidou in Paris.

He later suggested to me that I too should thank Derrida by commemorating him. It was this invitation that led me to write the present text.

Preliminary Note

Nothing seems more natural than for the living to forget the dead, and nothing is as obvious as the fact that the dead haunt the living. Of all the things said by Derrida with reference to his approaching death in the summer of 2004, the statement that occurs to me most often is the one in which he professed to harbour two utterly contradictory convictions relating to his posthumous 'existence': he was certain that he would be forgotten as soon as he died, yet at the same time that something of his work would survive in the cultural memory. These two certainties, he explained, both existed within him in an almost unrelated fashion. Each was accompanied by the feeling of complete self-evidence, and each was conclusive in its own way without having to take the opposing claim into account.

In the following, I would like to attempt to approach the figure of Derrida in the light of this declaration. It seems to me that this statement shows us more than simply a person in his fortuitously contradictory nature. Rather, through its unreconciled positing of two alternately valid observations, it has an expressive dimension that reveals something of Derrida's 'fundamental position' [Grundstellung] – if I might be allowed to apply that Heideggerian expression ad hominem just this once. Derrida's words amount to a self-description that almost has the character of a metaphysical statement. He thus concedes that in 'the real', whatever that might mean, there are oppositions that are incapable of synthesis, and coexist despite being mutually exclusive. Because these oppositions form part of the speaker's own thoughts and experience and determine him, this concession at once leads us to an observation about the philosopher: that he experienced himself as a place in which the non-unifying encounter between mutually incompatible evidences occurred. One could probably take this observation as a point of departure, and ask whether the tireless insistence on the ambiguity and polyvalence of signs and statements that is inseparably associated with the physiognomy of this author could perhaps have indicated that he experienced himself as the vessel or collection point of oppositions that refused to join and form a simple identity.

This comment could already provide the main outline for a philosophical portrait of Derrida: his path was defined by a constantly alert concern not to be pinned down to one particular identity – a concern that was no less profound than the author's conviction that his place could only be at the forefront of intellectual visibility. One of the most admirable achievements of this philosophical life is the fact that it was able to maintain the simultaneity of the utmost visibility and a resolute non-identity with any specific image of itself – in a shimmering parabola extending over four decades of his existence as a public character.

There are essentially only two ways to do justice to a thinker. The first is to open his works and encounter him in the movements of his sentences, the flow of his arguments and the architecture of his chapters – one could refer to this as a singularizing form of reading in which justice is interpreted as an assimilation to the unique. It would be an especially natural choice in the case of such an author as Derrida, who never wanted to be anything other than a radically attentive reader of the major and minor texts whose sum total constitutes the occidental archive – assuming one gives the word 'reader' a sufficiently explosive meaning. The other way is to move from the text to the context and locate the author in relation to metapersonal horizons that reveal something about his true meaning – at the risk that his own text may be assigned less importance than the larger context in which his words echo. This approach amounts to a desingularizing reading in which one understands justice as a feeling for constellations. Derrida himself clearly preferred the first approach and did not expect many favourable results from the second, as he knew very well that it was especially attractive for those who wanted to make him all too easy to deal with. Hence, when the occasion arose, he defended himself politely and clearly against Jürgen Habermas's attempt to declare him a Jewish mystic. In answer to this uncomfortable identification he remarked, with subtle irony: 'so I am not demanding that one should read me as if my texts could transport anyone into a state of intuitive ecstasy, but I do demand that one should be more careful about mediations and more critical towards translations and diversions via contexts that are often very far from my own'.[1]

If I have chosen, keeping this warning in mind, to take the second path in the following, there are two very different reasons for this. The first is that there is already no lack of ecstatic and literal, not to say hagiographic readings of Derrida to be found everywhere; the second is that I cannot shake off the impression that, with all the justified admiration for this author, it is rare to find a sufficiently

---

[1] In Florian Rötzer, *Französische Philosophen im Gespräch* [French Philosophers in Conversation] (Munich: K. Boer Verlag, 1987), p. 74.

distanced assessment of his position in the field of contemporary theory. This call for distance is an expression of esteem; for if one can also understand it as an antidote to the dangers of a cultic reception, it is all the more necessary in order to develop an image of the mountain range from which la montagne Derrida rises up as one of the highest peaks. In the following I shall sketch seven vignettes examining this thinker in relation to authors from recent tradition and the present day: Niklas Luhmann, Sigmund Freud, Thomas Mann, Franz Borkenau, Régis Debray, Georg Wilhelm Friedrich Hegel and Boris Groys.

1 | Luhmann and Derrida

Of all the constellations in which Derrida's work could be placed, the one involving Luhmann's œuvre is the most outlandish – but also the most revealing. Each of the two thinkers has been honoured with the highest and most problematic praise that can be bestowed upon an author in the field of theory: that he was the Hegel of the twentieth century. Titles of this kind may be attractive for superficial reflection and useful for public relations, but they can hardly accompany any serious interest. None the less, they possess a certain characterizing power in the case of both these eminent figures, in so far as 'Hegel' is not simply a proper name, but also refers to a programme or a position in an educational process. To mention Hegel is to speak of culmination, the *non plus ultra* and exhaustion; at the same time, the name stands for synthetic and encyclopedic energies that can only appear in the calm after the storm – or, as Kojève and Queneau might have put it, on the Sunday after history. These names mark a confluence of imperial and archival ambitions.

It would obviously be completely pointless to examine Derrida and Luhmann in terms of their respectively unique Hegelianism. Nor were the two men Sunday thinkers, but rather the opposite: tireless workers who made Sunday a working day – literally and for fundamental reasons – and furthermore held the conviction that on holidays, one either takes care of private correspondence or remains silent. What can be said is that both thinkers were concerned with completion and, while conveying the appearance of innovation, were perfecting and retouching the finished image of a tradition that could not be extended any further. There is a certain irony in the fact that, as we can see today, all those who thought that deconstruction and systems theory – constructs that emerged with a distinct profile from the 1970s on – had ushered in a new age of thought that opened up unlimited horizons for theoretical work were mistaken. In reality, both conceptual approaches were the finished result of logical processes that had shaped the thought of the nineteenth and twentieth centuries. In the case of Derrida, this involved the conclusion of the linguistic or semiological turn according to which the twentieth century had belonged to the philosophies of language and writing; in the case of Luhmann, on the other hand, it was the completion of the abandonment of philosophy called for by Wittgenstein, achieved through a resolute withdrawal of thought from the tradition of philosophies of the spirit and language in order to reposition themselves in the field of metabiology, the general logic of differences between system and environment. What both effects have in common with the case of Hegel is that they use the final possibilities of a given grammar to the full, and thus give their successors the initially euphoric feeling of starting at a high point. This subsequently gives way to the alarming realization that if one starts at the peak, the only way to continue is downwards.

In all other respects, the differences between the two Hegels of the twentieth century could hardly be greater. A certain superiority on Derrida's part is most evident in the fact that – like no other thinker except Heidegger – he always operated at the outermost edges of tradition, and thus kept tradition, however fractured, on his side. This explains the incredible effect of his work in the academic world, where deconstruction proved to be the last chance of a theory that achieves integration through disintegration: by breaking through the boundaries of the archive, it offered a possibility of holding it together. Luhmann, by contrast, left the philosophical archive behind, contenting himself with the ostensibly modest title of a sociologist of world society. To him, the only significance the philosophical library of the Old Europe still had was as a reservoir of verbal figures with which the priests and intellectuals of former times attempted to grasp the whole. From the perspective of general systems theory, philosophy as a whole is an exhausted, totalizing language game whose instruments corresponded to the semantic horizon of historical societies, but can no longer do justice to the primary fact of modernity, namely the progressive differentiation of the social system.

It is regrettable that the two Hegels of the twentieth century did not respond extensively and reciprocally to each other; thus we have no comprehensive minutes of the virtual logical summit conference of postmodern thought. It would have been immeasurably exciting for the intellectual community to experience the two eminent intelligences of our epoch interacting in a situation of elaborated dialogue. As both Derrida and Luhmann were of an extremely polite nature, each would naturally have resisted the temptation to treat the other's work reductively, let alone cannibalistically, as is normally the case among rivals for the highest position in the field of intellectual observation. None the less, each would have had to attempt assimilating though not absorptive translations of the other into his own terms – which, with two such masters of scepticism towards the very concept of the own, would have proved a stimulating exercise, and the observers of these translations would have had the privilege of being able to observe the reciprocal observations of the most conceptually powerful observers. Luhmann certainly paid close attention to Derrida's work, though nothing is known about Derrida returning the observation – it would seem that he never explicitly acknowledged the work of the scholar from Bielefeld.

Luhmann saw Derrida's deconstruction of the metaphysical tradition as an undertaking closely related to his own intentions, in the sense that he saw the same post-ontological energies at work in it that drove his own systemic theory project. He openly admitted that deconstruction was and would remain a relevant option: that it indeed did precisely 'what *we* can do *now*'.[1] This means that deconstruction is a strictly dated form of theoretical behaviour – dated in the sense that it could

---

[1] Niklas Luhmann, 'Dekonstruktion als Beobachtung zweiter Ordnung' [Deconstruction as Second-Order Observation], in *Aufsätze und Reden* [Essays and Speeches], ed. Oliver Jahraus (Stuttgart: Reclam, 2001), p. 286.

only appear on the scene after the conclusion of conventional theory's historical formation, and thus consistently remains connected to a 'situation' to which Luhmann assigns five attributes: post-metaphysical, post-ontological, post-conventional, postmodern and post-catastrophic.[2] Deconstruction, according to Luhmann, presupposes the 'catastrophe of modernity', which should be thought of as a shift from the form of stability existing in traditional hierarchical-centralist society to the form of stability found in our modern, differentiated, multifocal society. Once multifocality is taken as a point of departure, all theory moves to the level of second-order observation: one no longer attempts a direct description of the world, but rather re-describes – and thus deconstructs – existing descriptions of the world. One could say that Luhmann honoured Derrida by crediting him with the achievement of finding a solution to the fundamental logical task of the postmodern situation: switching from

[2] Ibid., p. 286.

stability through centring and solid foundations to stability through greater flexibility and decentring. With a sure feeling for the latent pathos of deconstruction, Luhmann adds the following to his concluding acknowledgement: 'Thus understood, deconstruction will survive its own deconstruction as the most relevant description of modern society's self-description.'[3]

The decisive element here is the seemingly harmless verb 'survive'. In using it, Luhmann may have touched on the motivational core of the other Hegel's work. One could indeed think that Derrida devoted his ambition to the development of a form of theory that would always have a future and the potential to become a tradition; this would be achieved by permitting and even demanding an application to itself, in the certainty that it would always emerge from such a test in a regenerated and re-consolidated state. This trick could only be pulled off by a theory that was always already lying in its own grave, so to speak,

[3] Ibid., p. 291.

rising from it only for repeated burials. Could it be that the core impulse of deconstruction was to pursue a project of construction with the aim of creating an undeconstructible survival machine?

2 | Sigmund Freud and Derrida

Such questions, which are really suggestions, put one in a dreamlike frame of mind. In its inner drift one finds the motifs of classical metaphysics re-establishing themselves as if under an associative compulsion. For me, a reverie of this kind involuntarily calls up memories of Sigmund Freud's late works. I am thinking in particular of the text *Moses and Monotheism*, which was written by the psychologist on the threshold of death and has remained a constant bone of contention since the publication of the first version in 1937 and the revised book form in 1939 – irksome to Jews, foolish to Europeans. As is well known, the first part – under the heading 'Moses, an Egyptian' – shows Freud developing the 'monstrous notion' that the 'man Moses, the liberator of his people, who gave them their religion and their laws'[1] was in reality an Egyptian by culture and nationality. In the second section, with the hovering title 'If Moses Was an Egyptian ... ', Freud develops the theory, carefully considered and bold at the same time, that the distinguished Egyptian Moses must then have been a follower of the solar-monotheistic Aten religion, introduced by Akhenaten in the fourteenth century BC, who, after the reactions of the priests of Amon, saw no possibility of propagating the unpopular new faith in his homeland and among his own people. Subsequently he joined the captive Jewish people to lead them out of Egypt – with the intention of resuming the monotheistic experiment in a new location with other people. Thus he taught the Jews the Egyptian custom of circumcision, the conventions of religious arrogance and also the strictness towards oneself that a strictly monolatrous religion must demand of its followers – or rather its test subjects. The ability to be

[1] Sigmund Freud, *Moses and Monotheism* (New York: Vintage, 1967), p. 3.

strict towards oneself is the source of the mental transformations summarized by Freud in the formula 'progress in spiritualization'.

In the context of a reverie there is a certain justification for bringing up this 'monstrous' revision of Jewish history by the Jew Freud, as it constitutes a manner of prelude to what will later be referred to with Derrida's key term *différance*. In Freud's interpretation, this 'shift' or distortion first of all concerns the real recasting of roles in the monotheistic game – but equally the redaction of accounts of this, which are always subject to the tendentious requirement of making what happened as unidentifiable as possible. Freud writes:

> The distortion of a text is similar to that of a murder. The difficulty lies not in carrying out the deed, but rather in removing its traces. One is inclined to give the word 'distortion' the double meaning to which it is entitled, though it makes no use of it today. It should not only mean to change something in its

appearance, but also: to take it to a different place, to shift it elsewhere.[2, 3]

Then *différance*, viewed in the context of Freud's comment, refers not only – and not primarily – to the break with a full present (as a temporal mode), but rather first of all – and primarily – to spatial displacement and redisposition in the casting of roles for a theological stage play. According to Freud, the true Egyptian drama is never played in the presence of true Egyptians from that point on. From the Mosaic intervention onwards, Egypt itself takes 'place' in a different location – while the literal Egypt, from the perspective of the emigrants, is no more than a dead shell that serves exclusively to indicate the necessary starting point of the escape to their own otherness. To be a monotheistic neo-Egyptian in the true Akhenatenic sense, one had in future to take

[2] Ibid.

[3] [Translator's note: this passage can only be understood with reference to the original word for 'distortion', *Entstellung* (verb: *entstellen*). The noun *Stelle* means 'place', and its combination with the negational prefix *ent-* indicates a displacement.]

part in the religious experiment of Judaism as conceived by the man Moses. Consistently enough this people, enlisted for a travesty, had to deal from the days of the exodus onwards with the problem of its uncertain territorialization, or – to use an expression Derrida especially favoured – it was chronically 'haunted' by this problem. The original content of his *hantologie*, namely the science of haunting by unresolved matters from the past (hauntology), thus becomes obvious (one finds this ingenious play on words in *Spectres of Marx*, probably Derrida's most significant political study, with a double allusion to both *ontologie* and Lacan's pun *hontologie*): it can only consist in the obsessive traces of Jewish-Egyptian ambivalence. Their origins had to be sought in the fact that Moses wanted 'to lead the Jews out of the country', as Freud says, and through circumcision impose a custom 'that virtually made Egyptians of them'.[4] With his analysis of hauntings, Derrida formalizes the idea, elaborated by Freud, that one

---

[4] Freud, *Moses and Monotheism*, loc. cit.

cannot be a Jew without, in a certain sense, embodying Egypt – or a ghost thereof.

This late work by Freud is not only notable for its development of the concept of 'distortion'; it is even more impressive through the inexorable consistency with which it 'deconstructs' the myth of the exodus. Read in the context of Freud's speculations, the term 'exodus' now no longer refers to the secession of Judaism from foreign rule by the Egyptians, but to the realization of the most radical Egypticism by Jewish means. From that point on, the history of ideas takes the form of a massive game of displacement in which motifs from Egyptian universalism are acted out by non-Egyptian protagonists.

What might be especially conspicuous to a psychologist here is that, in his final study, Freud barely referred to the concept of the unconscious in its established definition any longer – as if it had been rendered superfluous by the introduction of 'distortion'. One can view *Moses and Monotheism* to an extent as the self-correction of psychoanalysis at the last minute. The message of

Freud's late works would then be: ultimately it is not the unconscious that decides the fate of humans; what truly counts is the incognito that conceals the origin of the dominant ideas. Because distortion goes far beyond active concealment, it protects the Egyptian incognito in a way that is much more secure than the directorate of a conspiracy could ever achieve. Naturally the figure of Moses had to be the first to be affected by the distortion. Once it had done its work, the leader of Judaism was himself no longer able to say with certainty whence he truly came. In such a situation, projects become more important than origins. Now any consideration for descent takes a back seat to the prospect of the Promised Land.

If one pursues Freud's reflections on the cryptic fabrication of Jewish identity to their logical conclusion, the irreversible effect of the exodus becomes palpable: the departure from Egypt, according to Freud, spawned the Mosaic Jews as a hetero-Egyptian people that could not under any circumstances have returned to a previous sense of the own, even if it had desired to. The trace of the other had imprinted itself indelibly within the innermost part of the own, no matter how it might be disguised and covered up by new programmes. This imprint was so deep that even the symbol for the most intimate aspect of the own had been taken from the strangers: if circumcision truly indicated chosenness, as Freud tirelessly claimed, this symbol was borrowed from those from whom the Jews, as an emigrant people, would in future seek to set themselves apart at all costs.

3 | Thomas Mann and Derrida

At this point I am reminded of Derrida's insistence that one should be careful with translations and diversions via contexts that are often very far from his own. This insistence contains a distant echo of Nietzsche's well-known admonition: 'Above all, do not mistake me for someone else!' I admit that these indications will become particularly relevant in the following, where we shall venture a contextualization that exceeds the frame of Derrida's own statements about himself – and yet, as extreme as the defamiliarization may be, will possibly bring us very close to the nucleus of his most momentous operations.

I will take the liberty of imagining in the following that the dizzying career of the Algerian-born thinker – beginning in France, then continuing in the USA and finally in the rest of the world – was prophesied in an indirect, but personally apt manner by one of the greatest novelists of the twentieth century. It goes without saying that this does not apply to Derrida as an individual, but rather to the general type of the Jewish outsider who, coming from the edges of the empire, attains an eminent position in the logical power centre through dangerous and exceptional achievements. I am not unaware that a thinker such as Derrida, for whom respect for the singular meant a great deal, would have been profoundly suspicious towards attempts to understand the individual in terms of typical forms – none the less, I believe that on this occasion a journey in the sedan chair of the general type can also take us to our goal (or at least closer to the critical zone) without doing an injustice to the interests of the unique.

Thomas Mann became aware of the current relevance of Old Testament subject matter at a notably similar time to the aged Freud, and from the late 1920s on – as he later said in a well-known statement – he had set himself the task of wresting myth from the hands of intellectual fascism and remoulding it in a humanist form. One can assign his novel tetralogy *Joseph and His Brothers*, written between 1933 and 1943, a key position in the history of literature and ideas in the twentieth century – first because it constitutes the secret main text of modern theology, whose public emergence took place outside of theological faculties; and secondly as a grand parallel project to Freud's explorations in which Mann probed the immeasurable implications of a psychoanalytical and novelistic subversion of the exodus narrative. If the departure of the Jews from Egypt was genuinely a continuation of Egyptian culture by other means – and, in his own way, Thomas Mann reached similar conclusions to Freud – it could only be a matter of time before it would occur to the Jewish hetero-Egyptians to examine their connections to the homo-Egyptians, if one can call them that.

Thomas Mann found the pivotal point between the exodus from Egypt and the immigration there in the tale of young Joseph. As we know, he was the youngest son of Jacob, and his favourite – for which he was hated by his brothers; as a result, they ambushed him one day and sold him to Midianite slave traders in order to be rid of him. As the narrator shows, there is a profound ambiguity to this crime. It is not only suited to representing the secret of the injustice that is inseparable from preferential love and contributes to the birth of jealousy; it also provides an excellent opportunity to examine the problem of a revision of the Jewish relationship with Egypt, which was initially only conceivable as blasphemy. For the reader who is prepared to take the hint, Thomas Mann's irony supplies a hidden clue that, for a talented son of the progenitor Jacob, the best thing that could happen in his whole life was in fact to be sold to Egypt. Though this same Joseph could have become a respected shepherd at the fountains of Israel if his brothers had left him alone, or an olive farmer listening in pious serenity to the growing of the trees, there were other career options for him in Egypt – assuming the newcomer were able to turn his involuntary immigration to his advantage.

Thomas Mann's tale provides the most expansive commentary on the topos of a blessing in disguise. A sharp-witted hetero-Egyptian brought into Egypt through a second distortion could indeed have the ability to understand the homo-Egyptians better than they understood themselves. This hermeneutical superiority would be a gift bestowed by his specific marginality – and would in fact transpire to be the key to Joseph's successes in Egypt. Suffice it to say here that Thomas Mann's depiction, through a subtle parody of psychoanalysis, of the interpretation of Pharaoh's dreams by the young hermeneutician, who would soon become indispensable, is one of the most sonorous scenes in modern world literature.[1]

My suggestion that the novelist Thomas Mann may have succeeded in offering an involuntary prediction of the phenomenon of Derrida relates

[1] As I am developing a purely typological argument here, it is not necessary to take into account the fact that the chronology of the situation contradicts my interpretation. As the biblical story of Joseph takes place in the period before the exodus, the schema of 'back to Egypt' is not yet as applicable to the first Joseph as to the later protagonists in his position.

to the wondrous figure of Joseph – or rather the Josephian position as such, whose key characteristic must be revealed as that of being damned to success in Egypt. Having arrived empty-handed, the new arrival achieves his Egyptian successes, as we know, by a hair's breadth: purely through the art of reading signs that are unintelligible to the Egyptians – including, where necessary, the interpretation of dreams. What Thomas Mann had in mind was the career of Sigmund Freud, who, by suggesting a science of dream analysis, had succeeded in making the late feudal society of the Habsburg Austro-Egyptians dependent on his interpretations. Freud had made the Josephian position current once again in his own way, thus leaving his numerous successors a clue that the younger ones should not ignore. Naturally these authors no longer had to take the roads of the slave trade for their journeys back to Egypt; through the diaspora, the exodus became a partial change of direction for many. Even in modern times, however, one could only penetrate the logical and psychological citadel of Egyptian culture by no less demanding means than in Joseph's day: through the science of signs. Hence the interpretation of dreams is not only the royal road to the psyche; it is also the tightrope on which the hetero-Egyptian semiologist has to balance on his way into the inner sanctums of the pharaonic institutions. In doing so, he will realize from the outset that he can only try his luck by subjecting the symbolic fabrications of the powerful to an analysis that is sufficiently fascinating for them.

This is the right point to mention that Marxist readings of messianism such as those of Ernst Bloch and Walter Benjamin, only a generation after Freud, attempted the timely task of developing a second, non-Freudian interpretation of dreams. This did not so much revolve around the dreams of the rulers (and their wives) – these authors were rather concerned with realizing a mass interpretation of dreams in whose course the proletarian and traditional dreams of a better life would be elevated to a political productive force. The core of the second interpretation of dreams was the interpretation of signs and traces with which, according to the messianic reading, humanity had anticipated communism since antiquity. What was notable was the fact that the therapeutic restriction to nocturnal dreams was now laid aside, so that mainly daydreams and conscious utopian constructs were now to be integrated into the business of the new hermeneutics. Admittedly the case of Benjamin also shows how a Josephian career can fail against such a background. From Ernst Bloch, however, we can learn that the interpreter of dreams, if he has a sufficiently intense prophetic fire, is ultimately indifferent to whether the masses are interested in the politico-theological interpretation of their dreams.

Having presented these contexts, it is self-evident why Derrida's deconstruction must be understood as a third wave of dream interpretation from the Josephian perspective. For deconstruction it was clear *a priori* that it could only succeed if it went sufficiently far beyond the models of psychoanalysis and messianic hermeneutics. In keeping with the current state of affairs, this had to occur in the form of a radical semiology that would show how the signs of being never provide the wealth of meaning they promise – in other words: being is not a true sender, and the subject cannot be a place of complete collection. Derrida interpreted the Josephian chance by showing how death dreams in us – or, to put it differently: how Egypt works in us. 'Egyptian' is the term for all constructs that can be subjected to deconstruction – except for the pyramid, that most Egyptian of edifices. It stands in its place, unshakeable for all time, because its form is nothing other than the undeconstructible remainder of a construction that, following the plan of its architect, is built to look as it would after its own collapse.

4 | Franz Borkenau and Derrida

Returning from this typifying framing of Derrida's approach, I would like to suggest a further contextualization of his œuvre that brings us closer to the philosopher's text once more. This time we are dealing with a great tale of the responses of civilizations to death as detailed by the brilliant cultural historian Franz Borkenau (1900–57), a thinker with a wide-ranging interdisciplinary approach, in his posthumously published historico-philosophical magnum opus *End and Beginning: On the Generations of Cultures and the Origin of the West*.[1] The confession by Derrida quoted at the start, namely that he held two completely opposing convictions as to his continued presence as an

[1] Franz Borkenau, *End and Beginning: On the Generations of Cultures and the Origin of the West* (New York: Columbia University Press, 2001).

author simultaneously or alternately, reminds me directly of the fundamental theses of Borkenau's historical speculation. Born in Vienna and of half-Jewish descent, Borkenau had turned to communism early on after a strict Catholic upbringing; he was intermittently a functionary of the Western European office of the Comintern, then a fellow at the Institute of Social Research in Frankfurt. After his abandonment of communism he became one of the earliest critics of what he called 'totalitarianism' – his work *The Totalitarian Enemy* was published in London in 1940, more than a decade before Hannah Arendt put her stamp on the subject with the political best-seller *The Origins of Totalitarianism*. In his cultural philosophy he deals with the opposing stances of cultures towards death. While one type of culture rejects death and reacts to it with a doctrine of immortality, the other type accepts the fact of death and develops a culture of committed worldliness on the basis of this. Borkenau referred to these bipolar options as the antinomy of death. It represents the cultural formulation of the dual stance towards death found with more or less clear outlines in every individual: that one's own death is certain, but as such remains incomprehensible. Borkenau's ambition as a macro-historian was to use his doctrine of the opposing yet interconnected attitudes of cultures towards death to disprove the historico-philosophical doctrine of Oswald Spengler, who argued that every culture arises like a windowless monad from its own unmistakable 'primal experience' – today we would call it a primary irritation – flourishing and declining in an exclusively endogenously determined life cycle, without any real communication between cultures. In reality, Borkenau posits, cultures join to form a chain whose individual links are connected according to the principle of opposition to the respectively preceding link. This is the meaning of his references to cultural generations.

It is not surprising that Borkenau was unable to expand these ambitious concepts into a general cultural history. At most, he was able to give a reasonably convincing account of a single chain of cultural generations – not just any chain, however, but rather the sequence in which the main protagonists of the occidental cultural drama are involved. The series inevitably begins with the Egyptians, whose construction of pyramids, mummifications and extensive cartographies of the hereafter form a lasting and impressive monument to their obsession with immortality. The antithesis of Egypticism was developed by the subsequent cultures of death acceptance that we refer to as antiquity – including the Greeks and Jews, and in the second rank also the Romans. Among these peoples, enormous mental energies that had been bound through the work of immortalization under the Egyptian regime (and the Indus Valley Civilizations were freed up for 'alternative tasks'. These could consequently be used to shape political life in finite time – this may be one of the reasons why the invention of the political can be viewed as the joint achievement of ancient Mediterranean cultures of mortality. It is quite revealing that in this respect there is no real difference between the poles of Athens and Jerusalem, which are normally played off against each other. Both function according to the tenet that public life in morally substantial communities or among productively co-operating citizens' assemblies can only come about if the people are not constantly thinking about the survival of their bodies or souls in the hereafter, but rather have their minds and hands free for the tasks of the *polis* and the empirical *communio*.

The excessive grip of political citizens' assemblies on the lives of mortals inevitably resulted, according to Borkenau, in a new immortalist reaction – it led, with the mediation of a barbaric interlude, to the start of the Christian era in Western Europe. On account of its new emphasis on immortality, 'Christian culture' (though there is some uncertainty as to the aptness of the cultural concept) quite obviously constituted the grandchild of Egypticism, though it now made the immortality of the soul its focus – the Catholic cult of relics alone forms an indirect continuation of the Egyptian concern for the eternal body. But Christian immortalism, according to Borkenau's schema, in turn provoked its own antithesis through its excesses: the Modern Age, beginning with the

Renaissance, was once again a culture of death acceptance, and again led to the investment of human energies in political projects. (One of these, in keeping with the fundamental technical character of modernity, was the alliance of empowerment and facilitation of life, which would ultimately lead to the consumer society of today.) In the chain of cultural filiations, modernity would therefore be the grandchild of antiquity (hence *eo ipso* the great-grandchild of Egypt). Their common choice to accept death would then supply the deeper reason for the oft-noted resonance between them. It is in this choice that one would find the motifs that made a paradigmatic author of modernity such as Freud feel so conspicuously at home in the company of ancient philosophers – Stoics, Epicureans and sceptics alike.

The appeal of Borkenau's model obviously lies not so much in its capacity for historical explanation, which clearly remains precarious; nor would his aim of supplying an alternative to Spengler still be considered an attractive one today. What makes these speculative reflections on the antinomy of death current and fruitful is the fact that they do not present the transition from a metaphysical to a post-metaphysical semantics as a form of evolutionary progress or a deepening of logic. Instead they declare it the effect of an inevitable epochal fluctuation based on an objectively irresolvable antinomy, or an inescapable and irreducible double truth. Derrida's position within this fluctuation initially seems the same as Freud's, which positions itself clearly on the side of the modern extreme (and the ancient, Jewish and Hellenic cultures allied with it). What the philosopher calls deconstruction is initially no more than an act of the most thorough semantic secularization – semiological materialism in action. One could describe the deconstructionist method as a guide to returning the churches and castles of the metaphysical-immortalist *Ancien Régime* to the mortal citizens.

The strange thing about the approach, however, is that Derrida – to continue the architectural imagery – does not believe in the power of modernity's exponents to create authentic new buildings. (As his conversations with Peter Eisenman and the Viennese architectural group Coop Himmelblau show fairly unambiguously, he always remained distant from the world of modern architecture, and used such terms as constructing/deconstructing purely metaphorically, without ever developing a material connection to the practice of building truly contemporary, i.e. demystified edifices free of historical baggage.) He apparently had the same tendency, symbolically speaking, as people who are condemned always to live in old houses – or even haunted castles, even if they think they are residing in the neutral buildings of the present. For him it is clear that, even in the quarters of modern people, the undead from the otherworldly era walk in and out, just as the one God from Egypt never stopped casting his shadow across the huts of the post-Mosaic Jews.

In my view, one of the virtues of Borkenau's model lies in the fact that it helps to understand the complexity of Derrida's position a little more clearly. For, although Derrida paid tribute to the mortalist choice in the modus operandi of his analyses, the choice that is so characteristic of the Judaeo-Greek culture and its modern grandchild, he always retained a connection to Egyptian immortalism, and to a much lesser extent also the Christian form. This connection did not revolve purely around enlightenment or exorcism, however. Derrida did not simply want to drive away the ghosts of the immortalist past; he was rather concerned with revealing the profound ambivalence resulting from the realization that both choices are equally possible and equally powerful. Hence the pathos of his confessions, according to which one could never fully leave the realm of metaphysics. Essentially, however, Derrida always insists on his right always to retain his metaphysical incognito; he does not want an entry in his passport under 'unchangeable features' reading 'Jewish denier of immortality' – let alone 'crypto-Egyptian follower of overcoming of death'.

One can, in a certain sense, therefore regard Derrida as a philosopher of freedom, though certainly not in the tradition of Old European idealisms.

37

His discreet idea of freedom is inseparable from the effort to withdraw constantly from the initially inevitable identifications and pinnings-down associated with the use of certain idioms – which, incidentally, is why some readers seek to label him a neo-sceptic who, like the members of that school, declared a state of suspension between different opinions the highest intellectual virtue. If scepticism initially expresses no more than a reluctance to choose between the dogmatic teaching systems of antiquity (the Platonic, the Aristotelian, the Stoic and the Epicurean), then Derrida is more than a mere sceptic. His constitutive fluctuation relates not to alternative philosophical doctrines, but rather to the pre-philosophical choice of the antinomy of death; and this fluctuation incorporates the simultaneously necessary and impossible choice between metaphysics and non-metaphysics.

The word 'fluctuation' should not, of course, be taken as a reference to personal indecision – it is rather an indication that the situation involves a choice whose opposing options can be viewed from both sides by the chooser. When the thinker chooses, he not only senses the injustice he has done towards the rejected option; he also notices that the trap around him is closing. Whoever chooses exposes themselves to the risk of identification, which is precisely what Derrida was always most concerned to avoid. Perhaps one could view deconstruction primarily as a method of defending intelligence against the consequences of one-sidedness. It would then amount to an attempt to combine membership in the modern city of mortals with an option in favour of Egyptian immortalism.

If the deconstructionist use of intelligence is a preventative measure against one-sidedness, however, its successful application becomes particularly important when preparing for one's own end. For Derrida, who, as an unidentified thinking object, was always ready to answer to his students, friends and opponents as a present partner, the preservation of this sovereign indecision came at the price of having to keep the option of a double burial open for himself, for the time of his absence. One would take place in the earth of the country he had inhabited critically, the other in a colossal pyramid that he himself had built in a lifetime's work on the edge of the desert of letters.

5 | Régis Debray and Derrida

Since the death of Hegel, talk of the end of philosophy has become a fixed topos in the continuing discourse on philosophy. In the post-Hegelian context, the word 'end' primarily denoted completion and exhaustion. Later thinkers thus only seemed to have a choice between coming to terms with their epigonal situation or becoming original by doing something entirely different. Around 1900, the emergence of the philosophies of life marked an attempt to overcome this dichotomy – now thinkers wanted to combine spirit-philosophical epigonality with originality in terms of the vital substrate of thought: life. In this manner, the vitalists believed they could save philosophy by taking leave of it philosophically. It is well known how Heidegger's intervention ruptured this approach in order to deprive the thesis of the end of philosophy of its fatal significance. What had truly come to an end, according to Heidegger, was the era of philosophy as metaphysics or ontotheology. An older and younger approach than metaphysics, however, would be thought of as asking after the meaning of being. The destruction of metaphysics was not simply intended to open up the possibility of a different beginning of thought deeper in the past, but also to enable a different continuation of thought in a more current currentness. At its centre Heidegger finds the doing and the suffering of language, interpreting substantial language as the commanding proclamation of being. Hence [Gadamer's] statement: 'Being that can be understood is language' – for the sake of clarity, one should probably say: 'Being that can be obeyed is language.' Hence one encounters in Heidegger a metaphysically coloured form of the linguistic turn that dominated the philosophy of the twentieth century. As we know, Derrida, by turning from the philosophy of language to the philosophy of writing, also uncovered remains of a metaphysics of presence in Heidegger's project – he revealed the idealism of being-centred thought as a final metaphysics of the strong sender, and it was probably only through this that he brought the series of philosophy's terminations by means of philosophy to an end. From that point on, we read the texts of the history of ideas as orders that we can no longer obey. On one occasion, Derrida remarks that his basic stance towards the texts and voices of the classics is determined by 'a bizarre mixture of responsibility and irreverence' – the most perfect description of the post-authoritarian receptivity that characterized Derrida's ethics of reading.

Among the contemporary authors who acted on this situation, Régis Debray is one who stands out especially. He seems to have understood before many others that the business of philosophy demanded a paradigm shift. If the last word of philosophy, driven to its limits, had been 'writing', then the next word in thought would have to be 'medium'. By founding the French school of mediology – which differs from the slightly older

Canadian school through its more deep-seated political orientation, but shares a sense of the weight of religion as a historical medium of social synthesis – he not only provided post-philosophical thought with a new material horizon, but also established the vital connection to culture-scientific research and the theoretical sciences of symbolically communicating systems. Debray is therefore a useful adviser if the concern is to locate the phenomenon of Derrida within the cognitive household of postmodern knowledge economies.

To me, Debray's 2001 book *God: An Itinerary*[1] contains the most important hint at a mediological re-contextualization of Derrida. This is not the place to pay tribute to the genre of what one might call theo-biographical discourse, which Debray founded with his hybridization of theology and historical mediology – it is perhaps sufficient to say provisionally that he initiated a new type of secular, semi-blasphemous religious science which

[1] Régis Debray, *God: An Itinerary*, trans. Jeffrey Mehlman (London and New York: Verso, 2004).

44

provokes a comparison with Niklas Luhmann's 1977 work *Funktion der Religion.* (Whoever wants to distinguish such a functionalist-blasphemous approach from complete and poetic blasphemy should read it critically against Franco Ferrucci's distantly congenial book *The Life of God.*[2])

Naturally the migrations play a decisive part in Debray's account of the life of God, for the God of monotheism who is being discussed would not have any biography worth mentioning or describing if he had forever remained a God-in-residence, condemned to stay in the place of his creation or self-invention. It is thanks to the mediological intuition of Debray that we can now explicitly ask what media enabled God to travel. The answer to this can be found in an inspiring new interpretation of the Jewish secession from the Egyptian world. It presupposes that Debray's concept of mediality also incorporates the quality of transportability. The science of the religions becomes a sub-discipline of transport science.

[2] Franco Ferrucci, *The Life of God (as Told by Himself)*, trans. Raymond Rosenthal (Chicago: University of Chicago Press, 1997).

Transport science, for its part – or political semio-kinetics – becomes a sub-discipline of writing and media theory. Mediology supplies the necessary tools to understand the conditions of the possibility of 'distortions'. One now recognizes distortion not simply as an effect of writing operations, as declared by deconstruction, but beyond this as a result of the connection between writing and transport.

We are thus in a position to view the constellation containing the concepts of *différance* and 'distortion' mentioned above in a different light. If the 'distortion' of something, as Freud suggests, involves not simply a renaming, but also a repositioning, i.e. a shifting of its location in the geographical and political space, then one must, for better or for worse, understand the differing activity as a transport phenomenon. One can see how this can be conceived of concretely from the archetype of all transport histories: the account of Israel's escape from Egypt. The biblical exodus story may leave a great deal unclear – for example, the origin of the angel of death that visits the Egyptians' houses on that critical night while passing over the posts of the Jewish huts, which are smeared with lamb's blood – but it undoubtedly tells us how the first salvifically significant transport adventure was to be staged. The myth of exodus is tied to that of total mobilization, in which an entire people transforms itself into a foreign, movable thing that abducts itself. At that moment all things are re-evaluated in terms of their transportability – at the risk of having to leave behind everything that is too heavy for human carriers. The first re-evaluation of all values therefore concerned weight. Its main victims were the heavy gods of the Egyptians, whose immovable stone bodies prevented them from travelling. The people of Israel were able to change into a theophoric entity from that point on, *omnia sua secum portans* in a literal sense, because it had succeeded in recoding God from the medium of stone to that of the scroll. Debray writes:

> All of a sudden, the divine changes hands: is passed from the architects to the archivists.

From a monument, it becomes a document.
The Absolute recto-verso economizes a
dimension, two instead of three. The result:
the flat sacral (as miraculous as a squared
circle) ... Thus were water and fire reconciled:
mobility and loyalty, errancy and affiliation
... With the Absolute in safekeeping, God in a
chest, the place one comes from counts less
than the place one is going to, in keeping
with a history endowed with meaning and
direction. Without such logistics, would the
flame of monotheism have been able to
survive so many routs?[3]

We should note that the word 'survive' returns
here, a word that, as we have seen, belongs to the
central terms of the deconstructionist problem
field. If there is mention of a flame that must be
handed down on paper, we understand immediately how hazardous the operation must be that
will, in future, bind the eternal to the ephemeral
through the mortal becoming a vehicle for the

[3] Debray, op. cit., pp. 88f.

immortal. The abandonment of the world of petrified transcendences resulted eo ipso in a separation from the pyramids, which served as immortalizing machines for the great dead. So if the Jewish textualization of God involved his translation into transportable registries, it would be reasonable to suppose that the Jewish people may also have achieved a translation of the archetype of the pyramid into a portable format – assuming it still felt a need for the pyramid after the exodus. We shall now consult Derrida on the matter.

6 | Hegel and Derrida

No one who has even a passing familiarity with Derrida's work will be surprised if we feel compelled to modify this comment immediately. For no matter what we might undertake, we will scarcely be able to induce the inventor of deconstruction to make any direct statements on the matter of the pyramid. In the age of discourse analysis, as we know, any kind of directness has been abolished. A very wide range of authors have adopted the custom of not speaking or writing about a matter in their own voices, but rather via other authors who have spoken or written about the matter. This observing of observations and describing of descriptions characterizes a period that has turned the necessity of coming too late into the virtue of second-order observation in all areas. Someone regarding these logical games with a malicious eye could easily suspect that they show the nihilistic mediocrity of the commentators taking revenge on the genius of the authors of primary texts. Such a suspicion becomes unfounded, however, as soon as the first author is Hegel and the second Derrida. So if Hegel had been willing to make any first-order statements on the subject of the pyramid, we would have an opportunity to hear indirectly Derrida's thoughts on the matter. With a constellation of this level one can speak once again of an inter-Hegelian relationship, and even if it does not have the appeal of a direct encounter, it none the less shows the characteristics of a key scene.

With this scene in view we become third-order observers – and, as such, witnesses of a dramatic operation. It is like the final session of a drawn-out psychoanalytical treatment in which the last pharaoh of metaphysics is treated by its last Joseph. Derrida sits down silently behind Hegel, as is the custom, and allows the latter's monologue to unfold. Naturally the philosopher does not speak lying down, but rather standing at the pulpit of his university in Berlin, delivering the encyclopedia of philosophical sciences at the peak of conceptual power, bending slightly forward to do justice to his manuscript and the gravity of the matter. The deconstructionist analyst initially does nothing except listen to the metaphors, the leaps, the gaps and slips of the tongue, which possibly reveal motifs at work in this transmission of complete knowledge that sabotage its full closure from within.

Suddenly the tension mounts: Hegel has just begun to speak about the function of signs in the movement of the idea's return to self-presence – we are in the middle of the paragraph on the theory of the imagination or general 'phantasiology', an important chapter in the discourse about the subjective spirit. While Hegel is speaking, we see that Derrida, who had been listening motionlessly until now, is beginning to take notes. We can read these in the volume *Margins of Philosophy*, where they were published under the title 'The Pit and the Pyramid: Introduction to Hegel's Semiology'.[1] It

[1] Jacques Derrida, *Margins of Philosophy*, trans. Alan Bass (Chicago: University of Chicago Press, 1982), pp. 69–108.

immediately becomes clear: the fate of deconstruction will be decided in this scene – for when Derrida showed in his early studies on Husserl how writing clouds the diaphanous *entente cordiale* between the voice and the phenomenon, he had to clear the highest hurdle in his confrontation with Hegel in order to demonstrate how the materiality, differentiality, temporality and externality of signs obstruct the idea's return to complete self-ownership.

It does not require much effort for Derrida to show that Hegel's semiology is Platonically inspired: if signs have a sense, it is because their spiritual side equals a soul that inhabits a body – or which, as Derrida states with revealing caution, is 'deposited' within a body.[2] The inert body of the signifier is animated by the intention of the signified, so to speak. This animation is none the less assigned a strict limit because, even if the living soul is present within it, the sign as such remains irredeemably dead. The sign is a place in which the living directly encounters the dead,

2 Ibid., p. 82.

54

without the dead ceasing to be dead or the living ceasing to live – albeit in a mortified form, namely as a post-mortal soul. Signifieds would then be immortal souls following their interment in the dead signifier – whose deadness, however, testifies to the triumph of the soul, which asserts its primacy over the external material through presence in the foreign.

Thus the familiar schema *soma/sema* returns: the body, in keeping with the eternal refrain of Platonism, is the monument of the soul. If signs are monuments in which immortalized living souls reside, however, then one can see the pharaonic grave – the pyramid – as the sign of all signs. Hegel does not hesitate for a moment in drawing this conclusion. Semiology would then, in a certain sense, only be possible as a general science of pyramids – every encyclopedia would contain nothing but the avenues of vocal pyramids together with the written signs in which the ever-living signifieds are preserved, bearing witness to the hegemony of the buried breath over its shell with every single entry. Every sign, according to

Hegel, is 'the pyramid into which a foreign soul has been conveyed ... and is preserved' (*Encyclopaedia*, § 458). The decisive aspect here is that Hegel does not merely introduce the doctrine of the arbitrariness of signs that will later become the trademark of Saussure; this doctrine also takes on a philosophical motivation, for only through the random choice of signs does the freedom of the spirit come to power – in contrast to the heteronomy of symbols and symptoms.

From this perspective, it is not difficult to see why Hegel's interest in signs moves in a direction leading as far away as possible from Egypticism. If he is to bring his theory of the spirit to its goal, he cannot waste any time with the weight of the pyramids or the enigmatic nature of the hieroglyphs; both must be overcome, until the spirit can clothe itself in a shell of language whose lightness and translucence allow it to forget that it requires any external addition. This permission to forget is not a mistake; it testifies to the creation of a language that is sufficiently light and diaphanous to avoid placing any obstacles in the path of the idea as it returns to itself from without. In this sense, the Egyptians remain eternal prisoners of externality to Hegel, like the Chinese, whose language and writing form one giant system of barriers and disturbances that render impossible the fulfilled moment in which the spirit, distancelessly attendant on itself, hears itself speak.

It is unnecessary to show here how deconstruction treats these claims in detail. The basic operation of the third dream interpretation is clear enough: it consists in using minimally invasive gestures to relate the text of metaphysics to its inner dream drift, the delirium of unimpeded self-appropriation, and show its inevitable failure. It is sufficient if it proves the impediment that hinders this fulfilment fantasy. Therefore Derrida must develop a passionate interest in the Egyptian pyramid, for it constitutes the archetype of the cumbersome objects that cannot be taken along by the spirit on its return to itself. But even Hegel, the thinker in the age of light and seemingly surmountable signs, suffers the fate of being hindered in his final closure of the circle by a cumbersome obstacle. Even if the spirit's path through the cultures equals a circular exodus on which excessively heavy objects are left behind until the wandering spirit is sufficiently light, reflexive and transparent to feel ready to return to the start, there is one printed book left that, despite its handiness, still possesses too much externality and contrariness to be passed over entirely. Even as a paperback, the *Phenomenology of Spirit* is still an inert and opaque thing that denies its own content. As soon as someone points their finger at its cover and black letters, the celebration is spoiled for good.

Even the pyramid, however, will not be as interesting to Derrida as the dead king within it, as he is the only subject whose dreams are truly worth interpreting. One could even go so far as to say that a form of complicity comes about between the king and his dream interpreter; for in order to decipher the king's dreams, the interpreter must be able to dream them himself to a certain extent – although his main profession is the resistance to pharaonism and its politics of immortality. The deconstructionist philosopher is in constant danger of falling in love with the objects of deconstruction – this is the counter-transference in the post-metaphysical rapport. As a reading intelligence he is the victim of his receptivity, just as Socrates was the victim of the Athenians' gossip, which he absorbed into the breadth of his ability to listen. When the people of Athens assembled for discussions in the agora, the ear of Socrates was the agora in the agora. It is no coincidence that in one of Derrida's most brilliant essays, contributed to a Festschrift in honour of Jean-Pierre Vernant under the title *Chora*, he says the following about the proto-philosopher: 'Socrates is not *chora*, but if it were someone or something, he would resemble it very strongly.'[3] This bon mot contains, thinly veiled, Derrida's self-portrait: he characterizes the *chora* as a form of vessel without qualities, 'able and entitled to understand everything, and hence absorb everything (as we are doing precisely here)'.[4] It is

[3] Jacques Derrida, *Chora* (Vienna: Passagen Verlag, 1990), p. 46.
[4] Ibid., p. 56.

permitted for the deliriums of the oldest pyramid-builders to be absorbed into the comprehending soul of the deconstructionist, for there is nothing that cannot find a space – maybe even its rightful place – within this receptive breadth.[5] As a radical partisan of non-one-sidedness, Derrida wanted to call the dream constructs of the immortalists to order through the reason of mortality; with his reminder of the politics of immortality, however, he also corrected the blind mortalism of merely pragmatic reason.

We are still in search of convincing evidence that Derrida himself was aware of the continuity through which the pyramid as a real-estate venture remained connected to the Jewish project of giving God a mobile format. We find some proof in a passage from Derrida's meditation on the pit and the pyramid in which the author suddenly plunges into a dizzying speculation that goes far beyond the context. He has just expounded

---

[5] I am not in a position to judge whether, and to what extent, Derrida was aware of the similarity between his understanding of the Platonic *chora* and medieval theories of the active intellect.

Hegel's theory of the imagination as memory, which states that the intelligence is like a pit (leading vertically into the depths in the manner of a well or a mine) at whose bottom images and voices from one's life are 'unconsciously preserved' (*Encyclopaedia*, § 453). From this perspective, the intelligence is a subterranean archive in which the traces of things past are stored like inscriptions before writing. Derrida suddenly says something very surprising about this: 'A path, which we will follow, leads from this night pit, silent as death and resonating with all the powers of the voice which it holds in reserve, to a pyramid brought back from the Egyptian desert which soon will be raised over the sober and abstract weave of the Hegelian text.'[6]

What is conspicuous here is the reference to the pyramid 'brought back' from Egypt. The phrase is all the more expressive for being scarcely motivated by the context; it intrudes upon the development of the argument like a personal

[6] Derrida, 'The Pit and the Pyramid', loc. cit., p. 77.

declaration. It proves that Derrida thought of the pyramid as a transportable form – and the secret of this transportability undoubtedly lies in its lightening through textualization. But Derrida does not stop at this proof of the idea that not only the One God, but also the Egyptian tomb sets off on a journey: he now takes the risk of presenting the dream factory of metaphysics in an image of extreme pathos. Here, as he remarks, lies a riddle that demands to be solved, namely: 'That the path … still remains circular, and that the pyramid becomes once again the pit that it always will have been'.[7] How does Derrida know this? What is his statement that there is a way from the pit to the pyramid and back again based on? On the assumption that metaphysics as a whole, known after Heidegger as ontotheology, took this very path itself! For what was metaphysics if not the continuation of pyramid-building with the logical and scriptural means of the Greeks and Germans? Through this suggestion, which can claim the

[7] Ibid.

status of a lucid phantasm, the philosopher implies that there is a single possibility of deconstructing the otherwise undeconstructible pyramid: by transporting it back along the entire route it has taken on the trail of textuality, from Cairo to Berlin via Jerusalem, Athens and Rome. One only has to dis-distort it long enough until it changes back into the pyramid that it initially was: this pit expresses the fact that human life as such is always survival from the start. It fundamentally possesses the form of self-recollection. Existing in the moment means having survived oneself up to that point. At every moment in which it reflects upon itself, life stands at its own sepulchre, remembering itself – while the voices of its own been-ness sound from the depths. Whoever comprehends this understands what it means to integrate the ghost of the pharaoh into the sphere of brotherliness. One can easily imagine Derrida visiting Egypt and reciting Baudelaire's line *'mon semblable, mon frère'* at the eradicated monument to Amenhotep IV.

7 | Boris Groys and Derrida

According to Hegel's well-known schema, the path of the spirit through history replicates the path of the sun from the orient to the occident. It is inseparable from the success story of freedom. While only one person was free in the despotic orient, the aristocratic-democratic society of Greece achieved the freedom of a larger number of people, and finally the Christian West created a world condition based formally on the freedom of all. One could relate this movement a second time in the light of the reflections above, now emphasizing the politics of immortality – which results in a somewhat altered line. In Egypt, only a single person was immortal at first, and his conservation was the highest state concern (though one can already discern hints of later efforts to popularize immortality); in Graeco-Roman and Jewish antiquity there was no immortality for anyone; in the Christian era it was available to all. In modernity, a situation arose in which all humans were officially mortal once more, though relative immortality was *de facto* attainable for a number of people.

I would like to place this schema at the start of my remarks on the work of Boris Groys, which conclude this series of contextualizations of the phenomenon of Derrida – in the firm belief that it is especially suited to illuminating the post-Derridean situation. One can probably best describe the œuvre of Boris Groys, at least in its state so far, as the most radical of all possible reinterpretations of the pyramid phenomenon. Groys is never very interested in the question of how one can make the body of the pyramid transportable, however. He focuses exclusively on the 'hot spot' of the pyramid, the burial chamber within it in which the mummy of the pharaoh is deposited. If there is a problem of transport or repositioning for Groys, then it is only in the question of whether one can extract the chamber from the pyramid and install it in a different location. The answer is positive and surprising. According to Groys, one will never understand the artistic system of modern culture unless one observes how the pharaonic chamber is reused in it. The pharaoh's last abode forms the archetype of a dead space that can be summoned and rebuilt elsewhere – in any place where bodies, including non-pharaonic ones, are to be deposited for the purpose of an immortalizing preservation. The pyramid's chamber is thus likewise an object that can be sent on a journey – it especially likes to land in those areas of the modern world in which people are obsessed with the notion that artistic and cultural objects should be conserved at almost any cost. The Egyptian-style dead space is thus reinstalled wherever there are museums, for these are nothing other than heterotopic locations in the midst of the modern 'lifeworld' where selected objects are mortified, defunctionalized, removed from all profane uses and offered up for reverent viewing.

Groys too, one could say, is a thinker operating from a Josephian position, in so far as he – a post-communist emigrant of Jewish descent – brings the gift of marginality with him from Russia. He does not, however, derive any ambition to conquer the centre from it. Unlike Derrida, he no longer practises any dream interpretation in the textural power centre; he rather replaced the business of dream interpretation with that of dream curation. He is convinced that neither the dreams of the ancients nor those of our contemporaries require any new interpreters – there are more than enough of them already. What the dreams of the empire's inhabitants, their texts, their works of art and their waste products, require instead is original collectors and curators. The curator of dreams *eo ipso* deals more with the body of dream objects than their deeper meaning – in this respect he follows on from Derrida's onto-semiological materialism. But he is not sure whether he should give credence to Derrida's Romantic tendencies, his flirtation with eternity and absolute alterity – he sees in these figures something more like professional deformations that come about through a constant engagement with the fictions of the illuminated and immortal. Even Derrida's claim to the insight that there is no illumination is formulated too much in the mode of an illumination for his taste. Groys is extremely aware that Derrida, after Freud, Saussure, Wittgenstein and Heidegger, measured the boundaries of the philosophies of language and text, and was thus a completer. He therefore has no doubts about the quasi-Hegelian stature of the thinker – and is hence all the more convinced that the work of philosophy from the neo-Derridean position can only continue if its carriers change direction and do something else.

One could define the change of direction suggested by Groys in the après-Derrida in the following terms: where there was grammatology, there must now be museology – the latter could be termed archival theory. Groys is Derrida's Feuerbach – yet at the same time already his Marx. Just as Feuerbach comes back from God to real people, Groys takes the path from Derrida's spectres to the real mummies. And just as thinkers like Kierkegaard and Marx, who invented existentialism and the critique of political economy, were able to come after Hegel, Derrida is succeeded on the one hand by the political economy of heterotopic collections, and on the other by the alliance of philosophy with narrative literature – there are already examples of both today, and numerous other forms will develop in the course of the twenty-first century, with or without explicit reference to deconstruction and its consequences.

The sense in which Groys is to Derrida what Marx was to Hegel can best be explained using the concept of the archive, which plays a key role in the thinking of both authors. For Derrida, the archive governs the infinite within the finite; it equals a building with fluid walls, the kind Salvador Dalí might have designed – in fact, a house without any walls, inhabited by an infinite number of residents with unpredictably differing opinions. For Groys, on the other hand, the archive is a finite and discrete institution. It is not the imaginary, but rather the intelligent museum. This quality lends it a neo-Egyptian exclusivity. All that happens in the archive is that concrete innovations are constantly compared with concrete objects and assessed in terms of their collectability. Groys's archive is a funeral parlour for world art and world cultures – it is the place in which, as hinted, a number of persons can attain immortality with their works according to a law of selection that is never quite transparent.

The museological turn in philosophy must not be mistaken for a change to a different genre; nor does it have any characteristics of a flight to less demanding areas. It remains philosophical in the precise sense, because it reinterprets the most profound idea of metaphysics – the ontological difference as described by Heidegger – in the most compact of ways. The difference between *Sein* and *Seiendes* – previously between the eternal and the ephemeral – takes on a hard, concrete profile in Groys's thought: he now refers to the difference between what can be collected in the pyramid's generalized burial chamber, i.e. the archive or museum, and what forever remains outside of this chamber – the endless and arbitrary wealth of phenomena described with such terms as lifeworld, reality, existence, becoming, history and the like.

It follows from this that Groys cannot agree with Derrida's interpretation of the Platonic *chora*, as brilliant as it might be. Such an absorptive space without qualities is not of a psychological or introscendent nature, it is not the Hegelian pit leading to the interior, it is not like the hearing soul of Socrates, and it is not one with the wonderful patience Derrida has with texts. It is quite simply the burial chamber's dead space, reused in modernity as the showroom of art and culture. It is the space that interrupts the pitifulnesses of scattered life and the pretensions of becoming in order to enable contemplation. By visiting it time and again and describing it anew with amazing tirelessness, Groys, the philosophical commentator on the art of the present day, is in fact the last metaphysician. As a meta-vitalist, he enquires as to the transformation of mere life through its transference to the archive. Of all Derrida's readers, he is the one who honours him by leaving the paths of imitation and exegesis.

I would like to conclude this series of de- and recontextualizations of Derrida's work with a personal note. I will never forget the moment when Raimund Fellinger, my editor at Suhrkamp Verlag,[1] asked me during my visit to the Frankfurt Book Fair in October 2004: 'You know that Derrida died?' I did not know. It seemed to me as if a curtain was falling. The noise of the hall was suddenly in a different world. I was alone with the name of the deceased, alone with an appeal to loyalty, alone with the sensation that the world had suddenly become heavier and more unjust, and the feeling of gratitude for what this man had shown. What was it ultimately? Perhaps this: that it is still possible to marvel without reverting to childhood. To offer oneself up as an object for wonder at the summit of knowledge – is this not the greatest gift that intelligence can present to its recipients and partners? This gratitude has not left me since. It is accompanied by the notion that the burial chamber of this man touches a high heaven. What I have discovered since then is the happiness of not being alone with this image.

[1] [Translator's note: Sloterdijk's German publisher.]

Index

Index

Index

Index